BBC earth

DO YOU KNOW?

Level 4

ANIMALS HELPING ANIMALS

Inspired by BBC Earth TV series and developed with input from BBC Earth natural history specialists

Written by Camilla de la Bedoyere
Text adapted by Nick Coates
Series Editor: Nick Coates

LADYBIRD BOOKS

UK | USA | Canada | Ireland | Australia
India | New Zealand | South Africa

Ladybird Books is part of the Penguin Random House group of companies
whose addresses can be found at global.penguinrandomhouse.com.
www.penguin.co.uk   www.puffin.co.uk   www.ladybird.co.uk

Penguin
Random House
UK

First published 2020
001

Printed in China

A CIP catalogue record for this book is available from the British Library

ISBN: 978-0-241-35580-0

All correspondence to:
Ladybird Books Ltd
Penguin Random House Children's
One Embassy Gardens, New Union Square
5 Nine Elms Lane, London SW8 5DA

Contents

New words

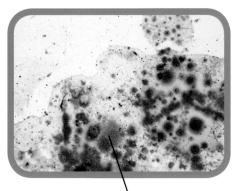

fungus
(fungi)

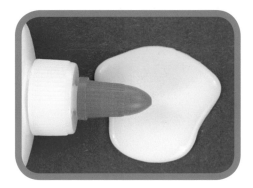

glue
(noun)

hole

honey

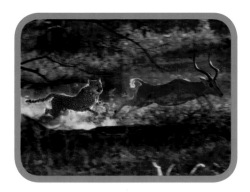

hunt
(verb)

insect

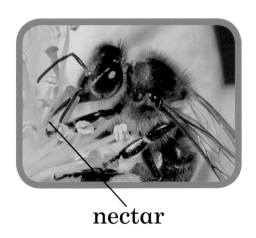

nectar

nest

pollen

shell

skin

Why do animals help each other?

Many animals live together in groups or families. They help each other to find food and water, and to stay safe.

Parents look after their babies.

These snow monkeys are cleaning each other.

This parent gives its baby food until the baby can fly and find its own food.

These bear cubs learn how to get food by watching their mother.

Clownfish and sea anemones live together.

They are different types of animal, but they help each other!

PROJECT

Work in a group.
Make a list of all the things you do to help your friends and family. Which three things are the most important?

Who looks after the babies?

Most baby animals need adults to help them.

Some animals live in big families. The families help to look after the babies.

A baby whale is called a calf. When the mother whales look for food, the family looks after the calves.

This sperm whale is looking after lots of calves. Their mothers are looking for fish to eat.

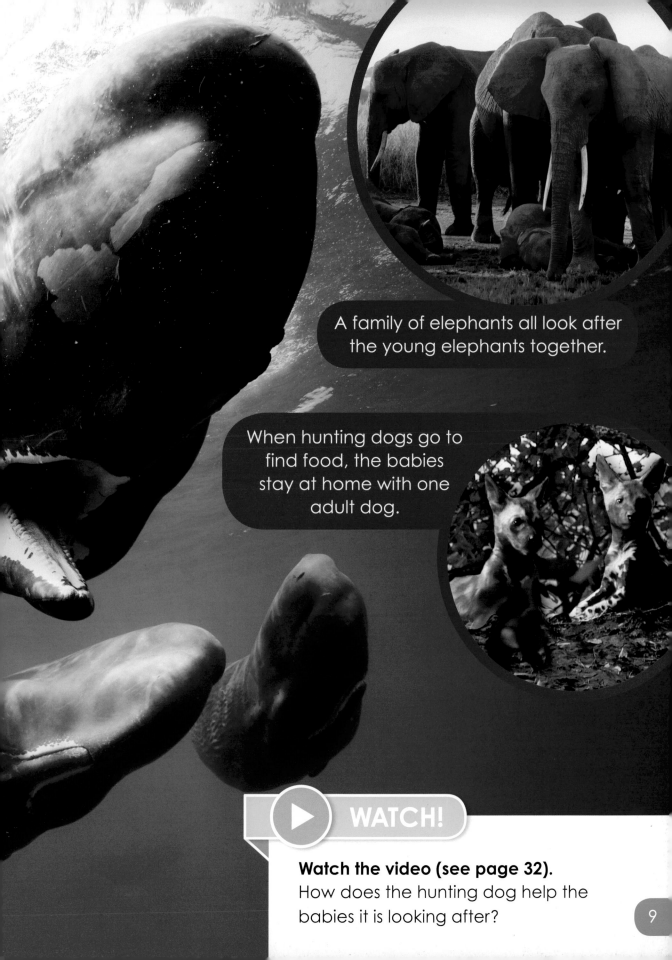

A family of elephants all look after the young elephants together.

When hunting dogs go to find food, the babies stay at home with one adult dog.

▶ WATCH!

Watch the video (see page 32).
How does the hunting dog help the babies it is looking after?

What are meerkats looking at?

Meerkats work together to stay safe.

A family of meerkats is called a mob.

One meerkat stands tall and looks around, and then it looks at the sky. It makes a noise if it sees a snake or a big, hungry bird. Then, the other meerkats can stay safe.

This meerkat is a look-out.

WATCH!

Watch the video (see page 32).
How does the meerkat keep its family safe?

HOW do groups of animals stay safe?

Some animals live in very big groups.
They help each other to stay safe.

Zebras live in groups called herds. If one zebra sees a lion or a hunting dog, it runs. The other zebras see it running, so they know something is dangerous. They run, too.

A big group of fish is called a shoal. They swim together when a shark wants to eat them.

The fish are bright silver, and they look like a mirror. A shark can't see all the little fish.

LOOK!

Look at the pages.
Which is the biggest group of animals – the zebras or the fish?

The ants keep the grass in their nest. **Fungus** grows on the grass, and the ants eat the fungus.

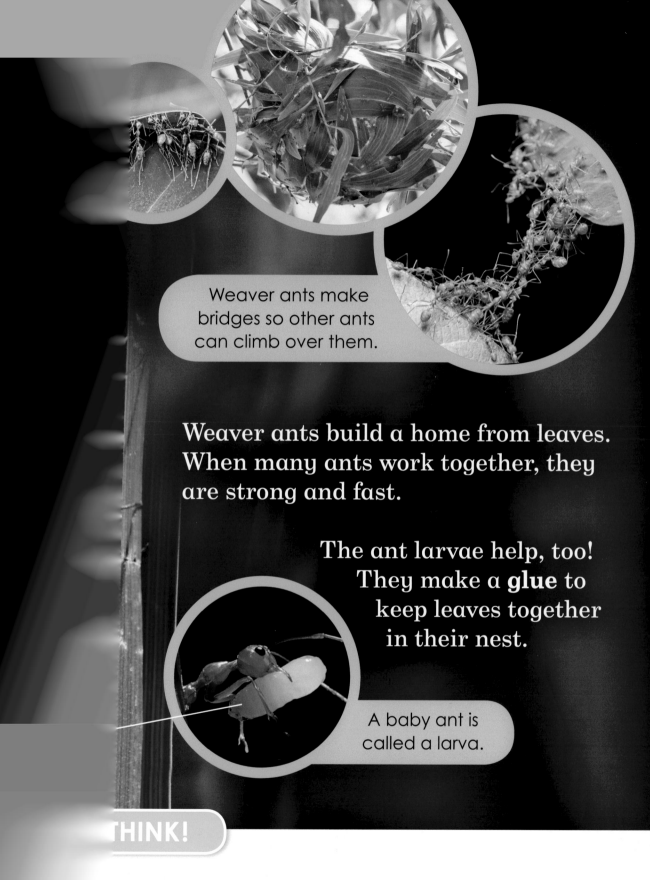

Weaver ants make bridges so other ants can climb over them.

Weaver ants build a home from leaves. When many ants work together, they are strong and fast.

The ant larvae help, too! They make a **glue** to keep leaves together in their nest.

A baby ant is called a larva.

...working together have different jobs to do. Which jobs
...ple do in your home or classroom? Make a list.

HOW do honeybees work together?

Honeybees live in groups called colonies.

Many honeybees live together. There can be 80000! Their home is a nest.

A queen honeybee is mother to all the eggs in the nest.

Worker honeybees look after the queen and her eggs. They also fly to flowers to get **pollen** and **nectar** for the colony to eat. They change the pollen and nectar into **honey**.

Honeybees dance to tell each other where to find flowers. Their dance is called a waggle dance.

LOOK!

Look at the pages.
What do honeybee workers do?

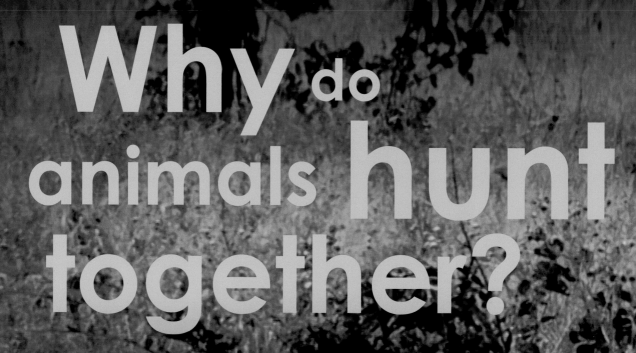

Why do animals hunt together?

Female lions work together to **hunt** big animals. When one lion is tired, another one will run after the prey.

An animal that hunts is called a predator. The animal it catches is called the prey.

Lions don't always catch their prey. This buffalo was lucky and ran away!

When animals hunt together, they can find more food. They can also catch bigger animals.

These young cheetahs are sisters. They work together to find and hunt their prey.

Cheetahs are very fast predators.

📖 **FIND OUT!**

Use books or the internet to find out what a group of lions is called.

Mother killer whales show their young how to catch prey.

Killer whales live in the sea. They make noises to talk to each other when they are hunting fish.

They swim in a circle around a shoal of fish. The fish can't swim away. Then the killer whales can eat!

A family of killer whales is called a pod.

Killer whales hunt together to catch big prey as well as fish. They hunt seals and small whales.

Killer whales are also called orcas.

LOOK!

Look at the pages.
Which three animals do killer whales hunt?

Can animals be friends?

Different types of animal can live together and help each other!

Under the sea, a grouper fish sees a little fish in a **hole**.

The grouper fish asks an octopus to help it.

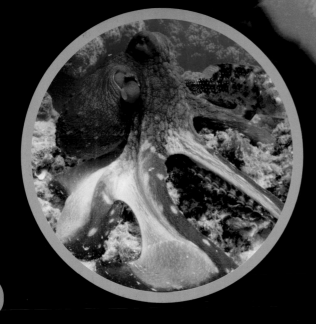

The grouper fish does a dance to show the octopus where to find the little fish.

The octopus has long, thin arms. They go inside the hole.

The little fish swims out of the hole. The grouper fish is waiting for it!

THINK!

How can you tell someone you need their help, without using words?

Why do clownfish live with anemones?

A sea anemone is an animal with tentacles. The tentacles have many little stingers on them.

If a fish swims into the tentacles, the stingers will hurt it. The sea anemone then eats the fish.

Clownfish live in the tentacles of a sea anemone, but the stingers don't hurt them. Clownfish keep the sea anemone clean. They eat any food the sea anemone doesn't want.

stinger

The sea anemone keeps the clownfish safe from bigger fish.

These jellyfish have long tentacles. Little fish are safe from predators here.

tentacles

WATCH!

Watch the video (see page 32).
What are the clownfish looking for?
What is in the shell?
What do they move together?

Which birds clean other animals?

Plovers are birds that help crocodiles by cleaning their teeth.

Crocodiles eat meat and fish. Pieces of food stay in their teeth, but plovers are happy to help!

The crocodiles open their mouths so the birds can take the old food.

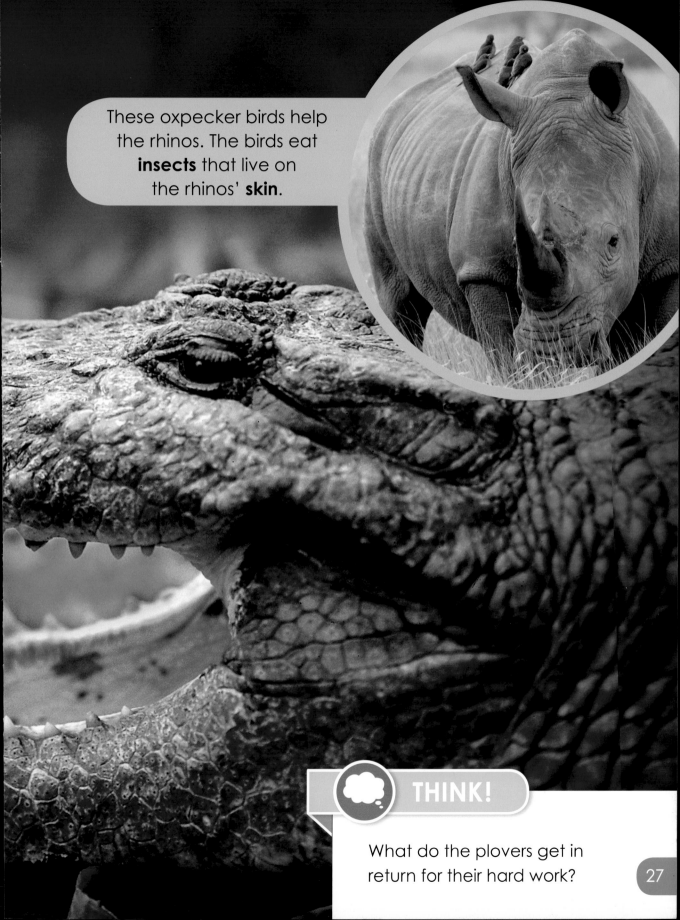

These oxpecker birds help the rhinos. The birds eat **insects** that live on the rhinos' **skin**.

THINK!

What do the plovers get in return for their hard work?

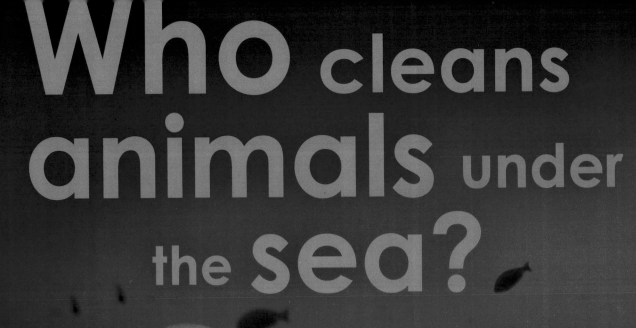

Who cleans animals under the sea?